Francine

By her dad

Dan Claus

ISBN: 1-933899-81-6

Published by:
Holy Fire Publishing
Unit 116
1525-D Old Trolley Rd.
Summerville, SC 29485

www.ChristianPublish.com

Printed in the United States of America and the United Kingdom

Preface

It has been 25 years since our daughter's accident at the age of 7. This is the story of her 7 months in the hospital and years of recovery at home. It tells of the miracles that happened contrary to all medical prognoses. It shares the joy she has brought to many.

This is written to give encouragement to others that are facing similar difficulties and weighing their options. It is also shared as a testimony to the goodness of our living God.

Thank you to the many people for their prayers and acts of kindness during our time of struggle.

Special thanks to my wife, Jane, for her help in recalling many of the details that happened years ago. It is difficult for us to bring back these painful memories of the past, particularly for Jane.

To our son, Craig, thank you for the help in putting the mechanics of the book together so the story could be published.

Our thanks also to our friend and neighbor, Therese Dandurand. for her helpful suggestions.

Contents

Chapter 1

The Accident

It was November 21, 1981, deer hunting season in the Upper Peninsula of Michigan. Our oldest son Steve and I were hunting out of the family camp while my wife Jane and our two younger children Craig and Francine were staying with my sister-in-law Nancy at her home.

This was Steve's first year of big game hunting. We had built a blind for him before season to protect him from the winter cold and conceal him from any approaching deer. During midmorning while half dozing, a nice buck walked up to him 50 feet away. When he looked up and saw the deer looking at him, he turned to shoot, but the deer swirled and Steve shot several times to no avail.

After lunch we returned to hunting for the afternoon. It was after walking for several hours that I sat down on a stump on the hillside which overlooked the wooded valley we were hunting. It had been a quiet afternoon, but all of a sudden there were several shots down in the vicinity of my son's hunting blind. I thought to myself, "oh good Steve has been given another chance at a buck". As I rested for awhile before making my way down to him, I heard some yelling then three shots and some more yelling. Then I realized there was trouble! As I ran toward the area my son was hunting, my thoughts were of an accidental shooting of someone in our hunting party. Oh God let it not be so!

As I reached Steve, I could still hear my brother Earl yelling for me and firing distress signals as he went deeper into the woods looking for me.

A friend of the family had come to camp with news that our daughter Francine had an accident and that she was taken to the hospital by ambulance. My first reaction was that she had probably fallen and hit her head in the basement as she loved to roller skate and was just learning to keep her feet from flying in all directions. "Didn't she wear the helmet we got her?" I questioned in my mind. My dad could see my anxiety as he tried to calm me with "it's probably nothing, you know how kids are". Steve and I set off for the hospital - a long 35 miles away.

When we arrived at the hospital emergency waiting room, Jane and my sister-in-law Nancy were there in tears. There was no need in telling me. It was serious! They were not totally sure of what happened but proceeded to tell of what they knew and what they thought they knew. One of the doctors came out from the emergency room and asked questions about what had happened. They were not sure if they were dealing with a blow to the head, a suffocation, a choking or some other cause. Nancy phoned back to the house to talk to Earl who in turn questioned the two children, our son Craig age 11 and his cousin Dianne age 9, to obtain further details on what had happened. They confirmed that Francine had suffocated.

Earlier that day the three children were playing in the bedroom. Francine, who was 7, asked the other two to roll her up in a blanket and roll her under the bed using a foam mattress to hide her. Jane and Nancy were not far away as they were housecleaning prior to going shopping. Jane peeked in on the kids and noticed Francine was missing. She asked where Francine was. They replied with laughter "over there under the bed" as they recognized their little prank had worked in fooling mom. Jane told them to get her out immediately as she left for the adjacent room.

Within a few moments our son Craig came out reporting to his mother "there is something wrong with Francine. It looks like her neck is broken." Jane, assuming he was kidding, went to take a look. Seeing Francine blue in color and lifeless, she screamed to Nancy for help. She told Craig to do CPR since he had just learned to do it in school. Again, Craig was only 11 years old.

Nancy rushed to the phone to call the town ambulance driver while Craig went over and started CPR. As he breathed into her mouth, she vomited, at which point Craig had to run to the bathroom to do likewise. Jane and Nancy then took over until the ambulance driver, Kelly, arrived with oxygen and other necessary emergency equipment. We were fortunate that Kelly just happened to be home from hunting and eating his lunch at the time.

Kelly, of course, was trained in first aid treatment. When he first started working on Francine no breathing or pulse could be detected. However, shortly after administrating to her, Kelly exclaimed "she's breathing". Nancy was then told to call a nurse who lived nearby and was also on the emergency rescue squad. When the nurse arrived a phone call was made to the hospital emergency ward to get further instructions in starting an intravenous treatment and insert a breathing tube down her throat. The hospital crew would then leave and meet up with the first responders halfway as it was a 30 mile drive to the hospital.

They would not permit Jane to ride in the ambulance since she was hysterical. Jane and Nancy followed by car behind the ambulance to the emergency room of the hospital.

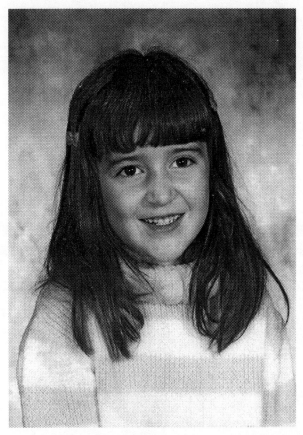

Francine prior to her accident

Chapter   2

Bad News Kept Coming

After several hours in the emergency room, Francine was brought to the intensive care unit (ICU) and stayed there for three weeks. During the first few days, we received information on the extent of her injuries, although much was withheld. We continuously had to ask questions. However, we could see for ourselves much of the damage. We were fortunate that a pediatric physician from the neonatal unit was filling-in and seemed to be very knowledgeable concerning what needed to be done for Francine. This doctor took charge and made things happen that may not otherwise have been done.

Francine was unable to breath on her own and was placed on a ventilator. She had aspirated pneumonia and her lungs had filled with infectious fluids. Tubes were placed into both her lungs to periodically suction out the accumulation of mucous. She had a hematoma (bruise) on her liver, most likely from CPR. Francine's heart was weak and rapid while her blood pressure was high.

They described Francine as being comatose and later induced her into a coma to reduce brain swelling. Whenever she opened her eyes, she had the most terrified look I had ever seen - more terrifying than any horror movie that I had watched. She had this look of terror for a number of weeks and it was heart wrenching not being able to help her. Due to lack of oxygen to the brain her body began to get rigid and after several days went into the fetal position. She became agitated when touched.

An intravenous tube was inserted to provide medication, liquids and nourishment. During one failed attempt at putting a tube into her neck they caused a large lump to develop on her neck which became a significant concern.

Francine was unable to control her body temperature as it often spiked to 103. She was placed on a cooling blanket to help this problem which persisted for a number of months but gradually improved.

Francine was in such an agitated condition that she would grind her teeth to the extent that she pushed out three teeth and fractured several others. She also chewed up her tongue causing a large split down the center. The appearance of her mouth became quite grotesque and had to be very painful. We wondered if it would ever heal. From lack of nourishment Francine became very skinny in a few days as she was thin to start with.

It was heart breaking for us to see our loving little girl in this condition. This was daddy's girl who would run to me when I got home from work, throw her arms and legs around me and tell me "Daddy I love you so much'. And now, they did not expect her to live. At best she would be a bed-ridden vegetable. Jane and I cried together. It would not be our last cry.

As I came to the realization of just how serious her condition was, I reached down to the furthest depths of my soul praying, "Lord, take her if she can not live a happy and healthy life, but we want her even if she is not normal". It was the darkest day of my life.

Francine was a very active, head-strong girl. She had a gang of a half dozen little kids in the neighborhood that she would lead around. They did what she wanted to do when she wanted to do it. Maybe her strong-willed nature would help her to overcome the severe trauma and illness she was experiencing? We looked for every possible ray of hope.

Francine did not like her name when she was little. It was too hard to spell for a kindergartener and it was a girl's name. She wanted to be a boy and be called Matt Lee rather than Francine Lee. When no one would call her Matt, she wanted to be called Super Frankie. So we would sometimes call her by that name. Like a boy, she was always climbing trees. More than once the neighborhood children would come running yelling, "Mr. Claus, Francine is stuck up in a tree". I would run to help her down and tell her not to do it again, but it didn't help stop her from continuing to climb trees.

One day, Jane received a call from Francine's teacher who tearfully told Jane that she was unable to discipline her. She said that Francine would tell her "you're not my boss, my mother is". Yet, at home she would tell Jane "you're not the boss of this house, Daddy is". When no one at home would comfort her after being disciplined, she would go into the adjacent room and cry, "My whole family hates me!" She was extra loud to make sure everyone in the house could hear her.

She loved to go to her Uncle Earl and Aunt Nancy's house and we had a hard time getting her to come home after visiting them. We saw them quite often as they lived next to my parents' house. Her

Uncle Earl once fixed a toy of hers and after that, Uncle Earl could fix anything. When something would break at home and I said it couldn't be fixed, Francine would say "Bring it to Uncle Earl, he can fix anything."

She also loved to be with my mother, Rena. She would go for walks with Grandma and often play cards with her. They were not the normal type of card games. They would both try to let the other win. When Grandma asked," Francine why did you let me win?" Francine would reply, "Grandma, I didn't want you to feel bad".

Francine's nature of being a strong-willed, bossy girl yet a very loving girl would be seen as she tried to fight the affects of her accident.

Chapter 3

An Uphill Battle

Francine was in ICU for three and a half weeks. During that time Jane and I stayed at the hospital around the clock monitoring Francine's condition and trying to help in anyway we could. It was like living a nightmare with one day running into the next and one week dragging into the next. We ended up sleeping on chairs, benches and on the floor in the waiting room for what little sleep we did get. We took turns during the night to go in and check on our little girl. It was exhausting, but God gave us the strength to carry on.

We farmed out our two boys, Steve and Craig, to friends and family during these three weeks and some other times during Francine's hospital stay. Our friends, both old and new, were a great help all through Francine's hospital stay. They made meals for us and supported us with their visits. Some of the women helped with the housecleaning and everyone volunteered to help in any way possible.

Francine was showered with get-well cards and gifts. Her room became full of stuffed animals. Cards and gifts came from strangers as well as friends and acquaintances.

Right from the start we had concerns regarding proper care of our daughter. An inappropriate toddler's facemask was used for her ventilator which wasn't adequate. It was replaced with an adult's mask that was too large, pushing into her eyes and irritating her. I asked the respiratory therapist to get one that fit. He told me that was all they had. I then said "then get a scissors and cut it down to fit her". He told me that hospital rules wouldn't allow that. I told him that I was going to call the doctor and walked away. I didn't call the doctor but shortly afterwards I went back to check and she had a mask that fit her.

One of the many unpleasant things that had to be done was to periodically suction out her lungs. This was extremely irritating to her and in an effort to make it as quick as possible I helped the hospital staff most of the time. It was not easy to see and hear her suffer through this process but it had to be done. This process continued for more than a week.

The antibiotic that was being used was not working as her white blood cell count continued to be high. Jane asked what they were using as an antibiotic and when they told her what it was Jane said,

25

"That particular antibiotic did not work on Francine in the past, you should try chloromycetin". Jane was told by the doctor that they were reluctant to use chloromycetin because of the potentially adverse side effects. However, Jane informed the doctor that this drug was used on Francine in the past and did not cause any problems. When Francine was 7 weeks old she had meningitis, went into seizures and almost died. We were told that she most likely would have learning disabilities in the future along with the potential for seizures. We never did see any effects of this. The chloromycetin did the job then and would help her once again with no side effects!

During the first few weeks Francine appeared to be in severe pain, agitated and horrified. The first time I picked her up to hold her it was like holding a skinny, rigid board. With time she did gradually have longer periods of relaxation. With time she also became less comatose. We had a hard time ascertaining her condition as the doctors either didn't know or wouldn't tell us, or more likely, a combination of both. From their negative reactions we were not given much encouragement. The only one giving us hope was the neurologist who said that the range of motion in her left leg was a good sign and "don't give up, you never know what God is going to do".

After three and a half weeks in ICU, Francine was moved to a private room were she continued to be closely monitored, tested, evaluated, and treated. Her breathing improved to the point of being taken off the ventilator. She had numerous blood tests, scans, x-rays; it seemed to go on and on.

Francine gradually improved. Her temperature spiking subsided, she had movement in her left leg, and she would visually follow in all directions and responded to some verbal signals. A mouth guard was fashioned to reduce the problem of grinding her teeth. We could see Francine fighting back in spite of her pain, giving us some hope.

Nutrition was one of Francine's biggest problems. Initially she was fed and medicated intravenously. Then she was fed through a tube in her nose (an NG tube). This tube was very irritating to Francine so they decided to surgically insert a jejunostomy tube. The jejunum is located just below the stomach. Jane did not want this surgery done and refused to sign the approval papers. I, however,

26

agreed to follow the doctor's recommendation and signed the papers. This was the first and only time Jane and I disagreed on any treatment for Francine. From then on, after praying, we came into complete agreement with each other on Francine's treatments many of which were contrary to the doctors strong urging or recommendations.

The botched procedures in surgically installing the jejunostomy tubes caused problems. The first tube was too small and plugged almost immediately. The second tube had a kink in it and didn't work. Each time the surgery was done Francine had to be anesthetized, her intestines stopped functioning for a couple of days, she received little or no nourishment, and she had to endure more pain.

We became disgustedly angry when the surgeon wanted to make a third attempt. We refused the services of this particular surgeon and insisted that he would not be allowed to touch our daughter again. He met with us to beg for another chance. The hospital administrator was with him. We gave him a very emphatic NO! To us this surgeon did not appear to "be with it". He had a blank and glassy appearance in his eyes. Was he on drugs? We did permit another surgeon to insert a third tube which worked fine for awhile.

After two months at the hospital in Michigan, Jane and I decided to seek a second opinion and try to obtain some kind of prognosis that we never received in Michigan. We were aware of the good reputation of the Rehabilitation Institute of Chicago which was a seven hour drive from our home but just an hour away from Jane's sister, Becky, were we could stay. Francine's rehabilitation doctor, Dr. Brown, agreed to this idea and made the necessary arrangements for the transfer.

Francine's discharge papers gave eight transfer diagnoses: respiratory distress, anoxic encephalopathy, increased temperature, increased white blood cell count, liver defect, mass on neck, weight loss and tooth fracture. Dr. Brown wrote, "We will be happy to take Francine back in transfer when you feel appropriate. Thank you for helping us with this most difficult and challenging little girl." This provided confirmation to our belief that they were lacking in knowledge on how to treat Francine.

Jane and I now looked forward to more encouraging news and

prognoses of our suffering sweetheart from the experts in Chicago. Surely, they will understand that Francine will make a great recovery and will provide guidance to aid in her getting well. We had great expectations regarding what we would be told at the Rehabilitation Institute.

Chapter   4

Searching for Hope

On January 18, 1982, Francine along with her mother was flown by air ambulance from Michigan to Chicago while I drove the family car to meet up with them at the hospital. This was the first time that either Jane or Francine had flown on an airplane, not the best way to be introduced to flying.

The route to Chicago was very familiar as I had lived in Calumet City, a suburb of Chicago on the South side, for three years after graduating from college. It was where I met my lovely wife and her family that lived in the area. The drive was normally a pleasant one with good roads except through Chicago itself. I had a road map of the city and did not expect to have a problem finding the Rehabilitation Institute.

The trip through the Upper Peninsula of Michigan and northern Wisconsin went through mostly forested areas where wild animals were often seen. The southern part of Wisconsin was generally picturesque dairy farms. We had made the trip many times both to visit my family when we lived in Illinois, and to visit Jane's family when we lived in Michigan. Oftentimes as we made the trip, Jane would remind me to keep my eyes on the road rather than watching the scenery or looking for animals. This trip to the hospital was entirely different. I was filled with good expectations of the news that we would have in Chicago and I was entirely focused on arriving at my destination.

I met Jane at the hospital's front door and as we went inside, we were met by one of the staff. She said to us "you're very lucky you have Dr. Gray who is the best in the country in her field". She went on to say Dr. Gray is a pediatrician/rehab specialist. This was very encouraging for us and raised our spirit of hope.

Francine was placed in a room with a little Korean girl probably a couple of years older than Francine. I would sit and have talks with her father and at one point he told me how hard it was to cope with his daughter's condition. That was until one day God told him that she did not belong to him, she belonged to Him and he was there only to take care of her. I never forgot what he said and I began to think the same way about Francine. But isn't that the way we should think about all of our children?

We spent ten days in Chicago, most of that time Francine underwent extensive evaluations and testing. In an effort to help

31

her with ranging her arms and right leg they did what was called "breakout casting" on her one arm as an experiment. Otherwise, it was observation and testing. The breakout casting was a procedure of stretching out an arm or leg to its fullest extent, putting it in a cast, and then cutting the cast in half. The cast would then intermittently be remove and placed back on for various periods of time depending on the patient's tolerance. After range of motion was establish to the degree of the cast, the limb was extended further and the procedure repeated until full range of motion was obtained.

Welcoming news was that her eyesight and hearing were good, but that was about the only encouraging information that we received.

They may have wanted to keep Francine longer but we were not favorably impressed with the loud and rambunctious atmosphere and, after our first extensive meeting with Dr. Gray, we certainly were not going to keep her there. Children were running around, seemingly uncontrolled, parents and visitors were having a good time watching TV with the volume on high and shouting to each other over the surrounding noise.

Dr. Gray pulled out a large book of brain CT scans and compared them to Francine's. She went on for quite awhile, pointing out the many scans that were of brains significantly larger than Francine's. Dr. Gray explained that these patients could not function; they couldn't talk, walk or anything, they were complete imbeciles. I commented that Francine was young. Dr. Gray said that makes no difference, the brain does not grow new cells. She went on to say "you see the little Korean girl in Francine's room. She's been that way for quite awhile and what can she do? She can move one arm and one leg. She has twice the brain your daughter has. How can you expect Francine to do anything?" Jane told her that we believe in miracles.

What a devastating prognosis! Our hearts sunk! This was the "good" news we were expecting in Chicago? We said very little. We didn't know what to say. Dr. Gray did all the talking as we shook our heads not wanting to hear her words.

The doctor went on to say "there will be a strain on you and your marriage. The care that she will require will not only destroy your relationship, but cause you to neglect her siblings and they will have problems. You will most likely end up in divorce. If you can not pull the tube and let her go, then place her in a home for the State to take care of her. She is not your daughter anymore. She does not know you and will not recognize you. "

Dr. Gray continued "I'm also Catholic and I recently attended a seminar dealing with life support systems. I can tell you that it is okay with the Catholic Church to pull her feeding tube. I didn't buy what she was saying but it didn't make any difference to us. We were not going to pull her feeding tube. How could anyone kill another person in that way? Talk about cruel and inhumane punishment! The doctor's parting words were "well, maybe some day they will be able to do brain transplants". It seemed as cold a remark as anyone could make.

We decided that Michigan was the better place to be. At least the physicians there didn't advocate mercy killing, although one resident physician at the Chicago Rehabilitation Institute did tell us "don't listen to her. She has no children of her own and doesn't understand. Francine will be your special child and bring you great joy."

The discharge report covered the problems of Francine's spiking temperature, her high blood pressure of 160/120, an increase of medication to prevent seizures, her bowel and bladder inconstancy, her limited range of motion in all four extremities, her oral defensiveness, and the atrophy of her left hand.

Chapter   5

Therapy Begins

We drove back to Michigan with Jane sitting in the back seat of the car next to Francine. We stopped only for gas and to use the restroom. Jane's sister had made us a lunch to eat in the car, but we didn't have much of an appetite anyway. It was a somber ride with not much being said. We both pondered the disheartening words of Dr. Gray, but we were determined to do our best for Francine and somehow God would help us. When we arrived at the hospital, Francine was re-admitted to the rehab unit. From then on the focus was on rehabilitation.

Upon re-admission, Dr. Brown, the rehabilitation doctor, wrote some comments regarding Francine's condition. He commented that, although she was very thin she was not in acute distress with her vital signs stable. He indicated that the problem with her neck that was caused by a failed attempt to insert an IV was now healed. He re-affirmed Francine's limited range of motion and referred to her as having clenched fists. Furthermore, he commented that she was neurologically alert and had sensation to deep pain. She had semi-purposeful movements in her left leg and moaning was the extent of her verbal skills.

When Francine was taken to her room in the rehab unit, we discovered that she had a roommate. It was a sweet little retired Catholic nun. When her Sister friends came to visit her, they of course, couldn't help but visit and pray for Francine. Additionally, they went back to their school and had their students pray for Francine and make get well cards for her. The nuns would drop them off at the hospital on their next visit. Francine's prayer base was expanding. Having this precious lady in Francine's room was a pleasant diversion from many of the unpleasant experiences.

Francine was started on a course of physical, occupational, and speech therapy. At least something was now being done to help her recover and it raised our spirits to some extent. Progress was very slow. Some of the therapist complained that Francine was uncooperative and that was the reason for her slow progress. Therapists with a positive attitude and high expectations made the most progress with her.

We would periodically have meetings with the staff that was working with Francine. Normally there would be about eight people in the meeting including Jane and I. Dr. Brown ran the meetings. A report of progress, or lack thereof, was given by representatives of each department. They also told of plans for future treatment.

At one of these meetings, Dr. Brown again stated his desire to cut the muscles in Francine's arms and legs so she would appear more normal. Evidently, he thought she would never have use of them again so why not make them appear better? He had talked to us a couple times earlier about doing this and we told him no. When he brought this up for the third time, I became angry, stood up, beat my fist on the table pointed my finger at him and said very emphatically, "You are not going to cut her! We talked about this before and told you we would not agree to that. We came back from Chicago with one good thing, which was the breakout cast that they did on her right arm. You see how good it worked. If you refuse to do it, I'll take her out of this hospital to somewhere that will do it!" Dr. Brown rather meekly agreed to do the casting.   Others at the meeting appeared to be shocked that I would talk to the doctor in that manner. Couldn't they understand our frustration?

It was rather amusing that some months after Francine's discharge we received one of the hospital's periodic bulletins that contained an article about Dr. Brown doing a seminar on breakout casting, as if he was a firm believer of this process all along.

Now I believe that Dr. Brown was a nice man and a dedicated professional but he was "over his head" with Francine's case. He was also frustrated with what he felt was our lack of cooperation. That frustration was shared by a number of other hospital staff personnel. They had even barred Jane from using the hospital library because she would look up information on the medications and treatments our daughter was getting and questioned them on what they were doing. How could anyone blame her for doing that?

At one point Francine began to have an unusual amount of hair growth over her entire body. She looked like a monkey! We were told that it was a side effect of the anti-seizure medication Dilantin. She was then changed to Phenobarbital. We were told that this condition would not worsen but, unfortunately, she would stay that way.   However, all that dark, extra hair disappeared sometime during her hospital stay. Who could we believe? What could we expect next?

The problem with Francine's missing front teeth gradually improved as the teeth on the side and back of her mouth moved forward and later on her wisdom teeth came in. Some years later we had a dentist perform bonding to build up one of the teeth that shifted to the front to look more normal. At the time Francine ground and pushed out her teeth from the earlier trauma she endured, she also chewed up her tongue. The front of her tongue had a large slit down the middle. We were concerned about the problems this would cause in the future but, her tongue healed rather quickly back to its natural shape.

We were fortunate that my sister-in-law's (Nancy's) mother lived just a few blocks from the hospital and had a spare bedroom. Jane stayed there quite frequently while I returned home to go to work and be with our two sons. I would often make the one hour drive to the hospital to visit Jane and Francine in the evenings and on weekends. It was a little difficult to concentrate on my job, but I did the best I could under the circumstances and everyone was supportive and understanding. I believe that my fellow employees were glad to have me back.

I never questioned our two sons about how they felt regarding Francine's ordeal. They're like me, rather reserved and not very expressive about their feelings. I had taken our older son, Steve, to see his sister while she was still in ICU and he began to cry. Right or wrong, it made me afraid to speak to them about her. From all the outside appearances, it looked as if they were coping quite well. In fact, they seemed to enjoy their new freedom from Mom and Dad's scrutiny.

The winters in the Upper Peninsula of Michigan can be quite harsh. One night as Jane and I were returning home, we wound up driving through a bad snow storm. On one section of the highway that borders the lake for about a mile, we encountered a complete white-out. I drove slow trying to feel the roadway but ended up going into a snow bank. By the grace of God, I was able to back out. I then had Jane drive the car while I got out and ran in front of her for approximately three-quarters of a mile until we got within the tree line and could again have some visibility. There were other times that the drive was rough but that one time was the most memorable. I was determined that nothing would stop me from being beside my wife and daughter when they needed me.

Early on during Francine's hospital stay, Jane asked the local charismatic prayer group if they could come to the hospital to pray for Francine. Jane asked me if it was okay since she knew it was not the style of praying that I was familiar with. I told her "It's okay. It probably won't help, but if it makes them feel better, let them come." After that, they came to pray with her on a weekly basis. People from our church's ecumenical charismatic prayer group also started coming, making the hour drive to pray over Francine.

The whole thing was a learning experience for me, forever changing my relationship with God to a more personal one. These people impressed me with their love of God and fellowmen. They were really dedicated Christians that expected great things from God. They gave us reassurances that everything would work out and God would use Francine for His greater glory. The pessimistic professionals could now blame these Christians for our optimism.

Francine's recovery was slow, but we saw continuous improvement. One night, before I left the hospital to go home, I leaned over to give her a kiss on the cheek. She turned her head and gave me a light kiss instead. It was as if she saying "I love you daddy, thank you for fighting for me." What a great and tender feeling! Another reason for optimism! This was a big moment for Francine and me.

Another sign of Francine's improvement was apparent as she became more aware of what was on television. At first she seemed to have little interest in it. We usually had cartoons on for her and, as the days past, we could see she was reacting more to what she was watching. During one of Dr. Brown's visits we told him about her reaction to the TV shows. He was skeptical and stepped in front of the TV to block her vision. She started to fuss at him. He stepped away and repeated to stand in front of her again as in disbelief. She got angry at him again. We told him, "We told you so." It didn't seem to make a lasting impression on Dr. Brown. He continued his negative thinking while we were buoyed in our belief of an extensive recovery for Francine.

Chapter 6

A Major Setback

Francine had been in the hospital for nearly six months slowly recovering when one day she pulled the tube out of her jejunum (abdomen). Orders were left to try to reinsert the tube without going through surgery. She was brought to the radiology department so that the insertion could be tracked.

A man, whether he was a doctor or nurse we didn't know, all we know is that he was teaching a group of students and was going to do this procedure. We'll just call him Teacher. He would not permit Jane to observe the reinsertion, which made her quite upset. Jane waited in the hallway. Shortly afterward, Teacher came out with a big smile on his face as if he had just completed the world's most complex operation. His entourage of admiring students followed him.

When Jane saw Francine, she said "that's not what you were supposed to do!" Teacher had placed a tube through Francine's nose rather than the reinsertion into her jejunum. He argued with Jane, "Yes it was" he insisted. Jane was furious! "Read the written orders" she said. Teacher read them and replied "oh". He had to go back and do what he was instructed to do. He was a good teacher. He taught his students how to make mistakes by not reading orders. He also taught them how to infuriate a mother by having a bad attitude. However, this entire episode would cause a more severe problem later on.

Some days later, Francine appeared to be very uncomfortable and in unusual pain. She had fluid backing up in her feeding tube and her abdomen seemed extended. When Dr. Brown stopped by to visit her, we called his attention to Francine's condition. Jane told him that she thought Francine had Peritonitis. He dismissed our concerns as, just Francine's "bad behavior" with the fluid in her jejunostomy as only bile. He assured that there was not a problem. Jane also talked to Francine's pediatrician concerning our observation.

We went home that night and spent the next day at home. Jane wanted to spend some time with our two boys and catch-up on some things at home. The next day we got up and made an early drive to the hospital. As soon as we got inside the door we were met by a staff person that told us "we need you to sign for emergency surgery as Francine has Peritonitis". The reinsertion of the feeding tube caused an enormous infection in Francine's abdomen.

She was rushed into surgery, and after several hours, the surgeon came out to the waiting room and told us somberly "It doesn't look good. Her infection was so extensive and so thick I couldn't even put in a drainage tube. I took out her intestines, cleaned them up as best I could, filled her up with antibiotics, and sowed her back up. If she should happen to survive, I will need to go back in and get the remainder of the infection in about ten days."

This was a major disheartening setback! We thought if we had not missed a day at the hospital, we would have forced some action a day earlier. We felt bad that we might have made a difference if we hadn't missed that day. But why couldn't the doctors see the problem earlier? They are the experts! They should have picked up the problem before us!

Francine was brought back to her room where we watched over her and prayed. That evening her pediatrician came to her room. He was aware of the bad news and was apparently there to try to comfort us as they evidently did not expect her to live. He sat down on the edge of the bed, but was unable to speak with tears coming to his eyes. We wound up comforting him instead and told him "don't worry, she'll be okay, God didn't bring her this far to drop her now." He left the room without saying a word. I should have been more upset and concerned than I was, but I had the feeling of comfort that everything was in God's hands.

I went home that night while Jane stayed by Francine's bedside through the night. Francine's temperature continued to elevate. There were no doctor's orders left to medicate or treat Francine for her high fever or any other problem that may arise, giving us further reason to believe that they expected her to die that night.

One of the nurses on duty said to Jane "I'm not supposed to tell you, but if we sponge her down, it may help". She could have been fired or reprimanded for what she did. So the nurse and Jane proceeded to sponge Francine down with water in an effort to cool her. Francine's temperature spiked at 105 then broke and came down to normal. The next day a white blood cell count was taken and it was normal. Any sign of infection had vanished! She needed no further surgery!!

We were very grateful for what this nurse had done. In general, the nurses were much more compassionate than the doctors. Most of them were mothers and had a better understanding of what we were going through. They would sneak and tell Jane what was going on and give her advice.

Unbeknown to us, our church had an all night prayer vigil for Francine that very same night of Francine's miraculous healing while they were unaware of Francine's trials and triumphs! Additionally, Jane had called her sister in Tennessee and they also had scheduled an all-night prayer vigil at their church that same night and they included Francine as one of their intentions. Don't tell us prayers don't work!

As we later read in Dr. Brown's discharge report, he makes light of the Peritonitis problem and other serious problems that were caused by doctors. There were some cover-ups most likely to avoid law suits. We did not file any law suits for any of the mistakes that were made on Francine, although we would have had good grounds to do so. I did threaten the surgeon who twice botched the jejunostomy operations. He sent us a bill that was the balance over what the insurance company paid. I told his office that he already received more than he should have and if he wanted to pursue it, I'd sue. The bill was immediately dropped. No lawsuits were filed because we didn't need any distractions from job #1, and that was our daughter's recovery.

Chapter   7

Accept Reality?

The hospital Chaplin talked with us numerous times, particularly with Jane as she spent more time than I did at the hospital because of my work and trying to help take care of our two sons.   He basically told us that our expectations for Francine's recovery were unrealistic. He went on to tell us that we should not expect any miracles, that God seldom works that way.

The Chaplin was a gentle and kind man, but for a Chaplin, he was a little off base. We believe that the hospital, primarily Dr. Brown, was behind some of his actions to convince us to reduce our expectations.

It was some time in the future, after Francine's release from the hospital, that the Chaplin approached Jane during a hospital reunion. He apologized for his actions and said he had learned a lot from Francine's case. He told Jane he had changed his approach and advice to others that he had since counseled. He was the only one that ever apologized for his behavior. It said something about the sensitivity and goodness of the man. What about all the others? Were they too proud or embarrassed to admit their mistakes?

One day, a gentleman stopped Jane and I in the hospital hallway. He said he'd like to talk to us about helping Francine. Of course, why wouldn't we talk to him? Anything to help our daughter. We went into a small conference room and he introduced himself as Dr. Green, a psychologist. I immediately thought to myself, "How can a psychologist help someone in Francine's condition?" It was soon afterwards that I could see that he was taking aim at us and our uncooperative behavior. After patiently listening to him, I told Jane "he's not talking to us about Francine, he thinks we're crazy. I'm not talking to him again." Dr. Green approached us a few days later and again asked if he could talk to us. I declined but Jane did visit with him for the second time. Afterwards, she came to the same conclusion as I did regarding this doctor.

Shortly there after, we received a bill from Dr. Green. I was irritated that he billed us, as we really had no desire to talk to him. Additionally, we had visited with a psychologist in Chicago but he approached us from a different perspective. He wanted us to take a break from our problems with Francine and go out and relax. He even offered us tickets to the theater. We never received a bill from him and assumed he was on the hospital staff just like Dr. Green would be.

I became particularly upset after talking to a friend of mine that had the same experience with Dr. Green. His daughter had received a brain injury a few months before Francine from a fallen tree that hit her during a storm while they were camping. Dr. Green pulled the same stunt with his family. My friend had become very angry with the tactics of this doctor and was protesting by paying the bill one dollar a month.

I decided to try to do something about this unethical practice of this psychologist. I went to the hospital administrator whom I knew a little since his mother worked at the same plant as I. I told him that Dr. Green was like a vulture roaming the halls of the hospital looking for unsuspecting prey when they were most vulnerable. I emphasized that if the hospital or some doctor was behind this, then they ought to pay this guy. The administrator told me he would try to get Dr. Green to drop his bill. He talked to me the next day and said that Dr. Green would not drop the bill.

It wasn't the money that I was concerned about. It was only $90. I'm sure my friend's bill was much higher. This was an unacceptable practice and I was going to stand on my principles. No telling how may others he entrapped.

After I refused to pay the bill I was summoned to small claims court. I didn't stand a chance! I quickly surmised that the judge considered me a deadbeat unwilling to pay the Dr. - a fine, helpful, well respected professional, a pillar of the community. As I went to pay his secretary, she said "you don't have to pay it all now. You can make monthly payments." I told her I wanted to be done with it. She said, "You know Dr. Green is a good Christian man who has helped many people." I responded with a sarcastic "yeah". I thought to myself, "I know a lot of "good Christians" who weren't so good."

Dr. Brown later writes in his discharge summary. "The parents remain very unrealistic with respect to her (Francine's) development and eventual outlook for recovery. After repeated attempts at getting them to realize Francine's serious neurological deficit they (we?) have given up for the time being. They are very resistant to any type of counseling, either from the clergy sector or from a psychological area. I think they will need some sort of support throughout this, but they are currently unwilling to accept this."

To me, expectations are the same as goals. And I've been taught in life and in my career to set goals high. If you set them low, you'll get poor results. If you set them high, even though you may not achieve them, you'll obtain much better results. This is because you take all the appropriate and necessary steps in an effort to realize your goals and expectations when they are set high. Time has proven this concept with Francine's recovery. Evidently Dr. Brown and some others on the hospital staff didn't buy into this concept.

Chapter 8

Going Home

After the problem with peritonitis we would not allow them to insert another jejunostomy tube. An NG or in medical terms, a nasogastric feeding tube was used through her nose. I was taught how to reinsert the tube because Francine would periodically pull it out and I would have to insert it at home. I became quite proficient at putting the tube down through her nose and into her stomach. In fact I did it a couple of times for the less experienced nurses in the hospital. I felt very comfortable with the idea that I would most likely be doing this at home for Francine.

Jane began working with the speech therapists on trying to feed Francine orally. It was extremely difficult and slow with little progress being made. She would push out all or nearly all the food with her tongue in a defensive manner. Jane didn't give up! When we eventually went home, Jane diligently and patiently continued the effort to get Francine to eat. We did not want her to be on that tube forever.   I admired Jane for all the effort she was going through. It made me further appreciate what a wonderful mother and wife she is.

Dr. Brown inferred that she would be on a feeding tube the remainder of her life and told us that at some point we would need to bring her back for another jejunostomy tube as she would not be able to tolerate the tube through her nose indefinitely. This made us more determined to get Francine to eat! We dreaded the thought of another jejunostomy tube because of all the past problems. There was certainly no reason to expect that the same thing would not happen again.

Prior to going home Francine was fitted with a partially modified wheelchair to hold her head, arms, hands, legs and feet in the proper positions. This was a temporary chair that was going to be loaned to us while a new wheelchair with all the necessary attachments was on order.

The Therapist gave us a list of specific instructions not to make any changes to the chair at home and why all the modifications were necessary. We were to check various spots on Francine's body for skin break down and she was not to be in the chair for long periods of time.

We told the Therapist that we were not going to order the special chair as Francine would not need it long. She was infuriated! She said, "Who do you think you are? We are the professionals with the specialized training. You don't know anything. You're going to hurt her." We calmly told her again that we wouldn't be ordering a wheelchair. We would go to the store and rent one for awhile. Still angry, the Therapist told us, "If you can't afford one, we can get Easter Seals to buy you one." I told her that our insurance company would pay for one if we wanted it. I did most of the talking for Jane and I, but like everything else, the two of us were in complete agreement.

We did not see any of the discharge papers until years later when our attorney obtained them for some probate court proceedings. So some of the details written earlier in this story were not known by us at the time of the discharges. From Dr. Brown's final discharge summary of June 4, 1982 we further learned or had confirmed more information regarding Francine's hospitalization. He covered what he considered six problem areas.

The first and largest concern dealt with physical, occupational, and speech therapy. Regarding physical therapy, Dr. Brown states that the only area in which she made progress was the result of her break-out casting (which we forced on him). Francine's poor behavior was given as the reason for not making any further progress. He also complained of Jane's and my resistance to positioning techniques in the wheelchair, saying that the parents feel it is not needed and Francine will become functional without the chair modifications. Who would be right, the trained experts or the parents that didn't know anything?

The negativism continued into lack of progress in the occupational therapy area. He claimed that there was limited success, again due to Francine's crying and pushing away. We could not understand why they expected Francine to react any differently. She was severely brain injured. We chalked it up to their lack of knowledge and experience.

Dr. Brown wrote that again, Francine made only minimal gains in the speech therapy area. He stated that limited success was made in the feeding program, but it was stopped because the parents were feeding Francine in the reclined position. This was completely untrue. We knew better than to feed her in that manner! And, we didn't stop!

The second problem that Dr. Brown addressed was the temperature spiking issue which was resolved during her hospital stay. I don't believe that they did anything about it except keep her on a cooling blanket and turn it on when her temperature climbed.

The third problem noted was some bleeding in her esophagus. She was treated with antacids to correct this problem. We were not aware that this problem existed until we read the discharge report years later. It wasn't the only thing that we were not told about. Why not tell us?

The fourth problem involved the feeding tube area and the peritonitis that nearly killed Francine. Dr. Brown claimed that the feeding tube in her jejunum fell out on several occasions. Not true! He also said that the jejunal feeding tube was reinserted after her bout with peritonitis. That's not true either. He wanted to put another one in surgically, but we would not allow it. How could he even consider another one after all the problems?

The fifth major problem listed was Francine's behavior. What more can I say about this that has not already been said? Except that Jane and I did not have major problems with Francine's behavior when we started working with her at home. In fact, when we made a game of it, Francine actually enjoyed her therapy at home most of the time. Also, the local therapist that worked with Francine did not complain of any behavior problems. She was a dedicated Christian and no doubt prayed for Francine as she worked on her.

Similarly, the sixth major problem given by Dr. Brown was the parent's behavior. I can't say anymore about this without getting angry, so I won't say anymore.

Dr. Brown wrote a discharge plan which included Francine being referred to the school district for a suitable educational program in September. In the meantime, she would be seen by a local Physical Therapist in our home community. Monthly follow-up visits would be scheduled with Dr. Brown and the Therapists at the regional hospital.

We took Francine home on June 4, 1982. We rented a regular wheelchair from the medical equipment store and returned the loaner chair to the hospital.

Chapter   9

Greed Doesn't Pay

It was obvious that Francine's recovery was going to cost more than our health insurance would cover even though we had good coverage and the insurance company was excellent in taking care of the bills. Therefore, I thought I should check into my brother's home owners insurance to see what they might cover as the accident happened in his home. I called my insurance agent to find out how I should go about contacting my brother's insurance company. He told me that I should not contact the insurance myself but I should use an attorney. He recommended that I use an attorney by the name of Mr. John Black. So I made an appointment to see him.

After I told the attorney the story of what had happened, he immediately started talking about a law suit against the mattress manufacturer. He told me of several multi-million dollar claims that had been awarded to clients of his. He said he could probably get four to five million for Francine. He told and demonstrated the extent through which he would go to win a case using props, charts, etc. I said that we were not interested in suing because no amount of money is worth ruining someone's life. The attorney replied "if you're talking about the other kids, no attorney would be harsh in questioning them and ruining their case." I said to him "this was an accident; it was the fault of no thing or no person". He told me "well we have some time before making that decision." At that point, Mr. Black started working on the case.

A couple of days later he came to the house to talk to both Jane and I to obtain more information. Attorney Black again brought up his desire to sue the mattress manufacturer and that he would use the insurance settlement to finance the law suit. He was probably hoping Jane would think differently about pursuing a suit. Jane and I both told him that we were not interested.

It wasn't long after that visit at our home that I received a phone call from my sister-in-law saying that our attorney had called her to get more specifics on the mattress and the accident. I immediately called Mr. Black and told him not to call my brother or his wife again and for the third time I told him there would be no law suit. I had doubts in my mind that a law suit could be won anyway and then the insurance money would be gone and we would end up with more heartaches.

It was ten years later that we found out for sure that the mattress played no part in Francine's suffocation. Working with one of her teachers on the computer through facilitated communication, Francine herself typed out that she had suffocated by rolling up in a blanket. Her brother confirmed what she wrote about the accident by saying "Mom that's what happened". Francine's teacher thought it might have been helpful for her to recall and tell what happened to her. The recalling of her accident and hospital stay did not appear to change Francine in any way.

The insurance company agreed to pay the maximum limit of the policy which totaled $51,000. When attorney Mr. Black and I went to probate court to sign the necessary papers, the attorney then pulled out a paper to sign that said he would receive one-third the money. I told him that was not our agreement. As I started to argue further, the Judge interrupted and told us to settle the matter outside the court room and come back later that afternoon. We set a time to meet shortly before our rescheduled court appointment.

I called Jane to be positive that I was correct and asked her to be with me for support when I went back to meet with Mr. Black. I also phoned a judge that I knew, told him the story and asked if Mr. Black was entitled to one-third the settlement. The first question the Judge asked was, "did you sign any paper?" I told him "no." He said "good, your attorney is not entitled to it. Stick to your guns!"

Jane and I met with the attorney Mr. Black in a side office of the probate court building prior to going back into court. He pulled a large legal book off the shelf, opened it up, and slapping it with the back of his hand, he said, "the State of Michigan says that I am entitled to one-third the money that I collect. It was my reputation that got you this money and I expect you to pay me for what I am entitled to." Jane and I both told him that our agreement was for his hourly rate of $75/hr unless there was a law suit. Mr. Black said he did not keep a record of his time because he assumed he was working on commission. He again insisted on one-third the money.

Finally I told him "look, I talked to another attorney and he told me that you were not entitled to it." Attorney Mr. Black flew into a rage threw the book on the floor and yelled, "I don't want any of it then. She can have it all! We're going back into the court room and I will tell the Judge that." We tried to reason with him and told him that if he didn't keep a record of his time to estimate it. An estimate would be okay with us. He refused, saying "and you can tell the whole community of how you put the screws to me." It really wasn't what we wanted but, we could see that he was not in a reasonable mood.

He told the Court exactly what he told us. Francine could have it all! He said he was off the case and flew out the door. The Judge and the Court Stenographer were smiling and as I went up to check on what to do next, I asked the stenographer why they were smiling. She said, half whispering, "We were so glad you didn't give in to him. He bullies everyone and few people stand up to him. We're happy that you did." I felt good that she confirmed that we did the right thing. She told me that I needed to get another attorney to finish up.

I made an appointment to see an attorney that I had met socially a couple of times. After telling him what happened he told me that attorneys normally don't like taking such cases leftover from another attorney. He had some legal profession name for it. He would do some checking and call me back. It wasn't long before he called me and said, "Dan I apologize for not believing you. I checked the court records and you were right. I'll finish it up for you." The cost was minimal.

When I received the money I stuck most of it into short term certificates of deposits (paying 11% at the time) then I talked to a friend of mine who was financially knowledgeable about investing. He suggested mutual stock funds for long term investing. Back then the list of mutual funds was a fraction of what it is today. Over the years the investments multiplied several times over while still frequently tapping them for necessities and fun things for Francine.

We used quite a bit of the money for respite over the years. Some of it was used for dental work which was not covered by Medicaid. The bulk of what was spent was used for such things as; going to movies, buying videos and music CDs, lunch with her caregivers, horseback riding, toys, a 4-wheeled ATV, a boat, and trips (including two to Disney World).

Chapter   10

Recovery at Home

We had prepared a place for Francine to stay in our family room where her feeding bag could be hung and she could watch TV and be a part of family activities. An aquarium was bought and placed by her temporary quarters so that she would have something relaxing to watch. The entire family pitched in to help with Francine's recovery. The experience brought our family closer together, particularly Jane and me. It was completely contrary to what we were told by Dr. Gray in Chicago, i.e. the stress would split our family and we would end up in divorce.

At Francine's discharge, the Occupational Therapist gave us some instructions along with some suggested logs that we keep. The first set of instructions was to record Francine's response to verbal requests. The responses had to be prompt, consistent and lasting. A daily record was to be kept of the foods/liquids, the amounts and types, that Francine eats/drinks. Suggestions were given to help Francine with her eating/drinking such as; putting foods on her fingers that she sticks in her mouth, using a straw and placing a cup next to her lips to desensitize her mouth and putting a spoon in her hand and bringing it up to her mouth. Francine was to receive lots of praise for things she accomplished and was to be ignored for things she didn't do.

Jane kept the logs and did the bulk of the physical therapy and feeding that first summer. I managed the feeding tube which on occasions had to be reinserted. Francine's two older brothers, myself, friends and neighbors did the fun things with her including playing games, going for walks in the wheelchair and going swimming. My niece came to stay with us also that summer to help out. We would use Francine's stuffed animals to talk, sing and dance for her. We would go through books showing her pictures of the things she loved like; animals, trucks and sport cars. As time went on, she became more attentive and showed greater enjoyment in our activities with her.

While Francine was in the hospital, all she would say clearly was "mama "and "help" when she saw the therapist. The day we took her home, as we put her in the car, she clearly said "home". Otherwise, she would speak very few words the first month she was home. She did learn to say "no" rather quickly, however. She also learned to say "up" soon afterwards as she wanted to be sitting up rather than lying down. Hi and bye were two of the next words that she would say consistently. Little by little, month by month and year by year,

Francine learned to say more words and eventually short sentences. Yet today, she says a lot of what we believe are words and sentences to her but come out jumbled. When we ask her what she said she repeats the same jumbled words. We are hoping that one day everything will be spoken clearly.

Jane patiently worked on Francine's feeding. By early August, two months after we brought her home, she was capable of eating and drinking enough without using the feeding tube. It happened suddenly over one weekend. So we pulled her feeding tube! In January of 1983, Jane and the teachers at Francine's school began working on a self feeding program.

Some months later, Jane and Francine flew down to visit Jane's sister, Frances, in Englewood Tennessee to get a change of scenery and to also visit Jane's parents who could no longer travel. One day as they were preparing to go out shopping, Jane asked Frances to get some cereal for Francine. After getting ready, Jane went out to the kitchen and saw that Francine's cereal was all gone. She asked Frances, "She ate the whole thing?" Frances said, "Yes, she sure feeds her self good!" Jane told her, "She doesn't feed herself!" From then on Francine fed herself!

Francine physically progressed as well. Due to the injury all the muscles in her body had atrophied to various extents. We were told that her left hand was so bad that she would not be able to make use of it. Tests showed she had permanent nerve damage to that hand. Contrarily, after about a month at home she began to use it. In fact it was the hand she preferred to use while she sort of ignored the right hand. It was not until approximately ten years later when her right hand swelled and turned red that Francine started using the right hand to any extent. At that time she was taken to a rehabilitation doctor who said the swelling occurred because the hand was coming back. The swelling did eventually go away. How happy we were. Another miracle!

On August 16th she slept in her own room. With her stretching exercises she reached full range of motion in her arms and legs. Her desire to sit up helped in developing strength in most of her body. After getting over her initial fear when reintroduced to the swimming pool, swimming was also a big help in exercising her entire body. She could swim like a fish prior to her accident, but afterwards she dog-paddled around the pool. She still loves to swim.

To develop strength in her legs, Jane and I began to hold her in the standing position for short periods of time. We started to do this two months after she was home. When she started school, they would put her on a standing board to strengthen her legs. After a couple of months of this, I came up with an idea that I was eager to try. I had a large pair of swimming fins that I would put on my feet, stand Francine on top of them with her back to me, walk with her in that manner while swinging her arms in the natural way when one walks. It worked! I later found out that this was a technique called patterning.

The next step was to hold her hand as she walked. Her brother Craig found a way to break that habit. He held on to one end of a plastic banana while Francine held the other end. He would then let go of his end and Francine would be walking around holding onto the banana by herself. Shortly thereafter she would walk without holding on to anything for security. To further help her with her walking, her brothers and I took her for walks outdoors and through the woods to get her familiar with walking on uneven surfaces and stepping over objects. By the spring and into the summer of 1983 Francine was walking quite well although she had a gait with a wide stance and sort of a shuffle in her walk. By that fall she was running but we had to be careful as she occasionally would trip and fall. To this day, she still prefers to hold someone's hand when she walks.

The injury left Francine both bladder and bowel incontinent. With time and effort this problem was nearly overcome by the fall of 1983, just a little over a year after her discharge from the hospital. For quite a few years now she has gone to the bathroom completely on her own.

Shortly after we brought her home, she started to pull on her hair. She got into the habit of pulling so much so, she became bare on one side. I was able to break that habit by giving her a butch hair cut so that it was too short to pull. When she went out we put a hat on her to cover it up. It was winter time anyway so her hair cut and cover-up weren't noticeable.

At one point Jane took Francine to her primary doctor in the community where we lived. This had been Francine's doctor for a number of years and was familiar with her. Francine had a urine infection to be taken care of plus we wanted her doctor to see her as she was different than in the past. The doctor was very cold toward Francine and acted like he didn't want anything to do with her. We did not understand this change of attitude. It was hurtful! Jane therefore took her to another local doctor who was very compassionate and happy to do whatever he could for Francine.

The first year of school Jane drove her there two days a week. Then she increased it to three days. The following year Francine started riding the bus to school. She liked riding the bus even though it was an hour and a half ride one way. The cooperation that Francine gave to the teachers, aids and therapist varied depending on how much she liked the person. The more positive, outgoing people continued to get the most out of her. In November of 1985,(four years after the accident) one of the aids wrote; "I was working with Francine yesterday and out of the blue she said " I like you" and gave me a big hug! We all got so exited! It made our day! It seems lately like she's just bubbling and really eager to communicate! Today at speech I was sitting in on her session and she pointed "walk outside" when asked what she wanted."

Francine went for physical therapy once a week at the local community hospital. She also went back for monthly checkups with the rehab doctor (Dr. Brown) for several months and with the therapists at the regional hospital. When Francine started school, Jane would sometimes take Francine to visit the hospital as the school was not too far from the hospital. Jane wanted the nurses and other folks at the hospital to see for themselves just how good Francine was doing. Most were happy to see Francine and how much progress she had made.

One day while visiting the hospital, they ran into the Physical Therapist that had become so infuriated with us for not ordering the special chair for Francine. She bent down and said to Francine in a very sarcastic manner, "Poor Francine, I see you're still in a wheelchair." Jane said, "Francine standup '. When Francine stood up, the jaw of the Therapist dropped to the floor in disbelief. She quickly turned around and walked away without saying another word. The Therapist realized that she had been wrong and was too proud to admit it. Jane was too modest to say, "We told you so."

During that same winter of Jane driving Francine to school, my mother had a near fatal accident. She was walking to visit a neighbor when she was struck by a hit-and-run driver. She was thrown up on the snow bank by the impact and left for dead. She was not expected to survive the night. She had massive internal injuries, a broken leg that was twisted to her back, a shattered pelvis, and was black and blue on nearly her entire body. She survived, had a couple of operations on her leg and at one point was scheduled to have some surgery on her hip.

Jane would visit my mother frequently while she waited for Francine to finish her day at school. The evening before the scheduled surgery, Jane and I went to see her primarily to pray for the success of the surgery. The next day new x-rays were done just prior to taking her in for surgery. They showed her to be completely healed! The surgery was cancelled! Another miracle! A few days later Jane ran into one of the nurses that was familiar with both Francine's and my mother's cases and, shaking her head in disbelief, said "you Claus' are amazing!"

We had another doctor that we wanted to show Francine's progress to, Dr. Gray in Chicago. A couple of years after Francine was discharged from the hospital, we went to visit Jane's sister Becky and her family who lived just south of Chicago in Highland, Indiana. While there, we stopped in at the Rehabilitation Institute to see Dr. Gray. When we introduced Francine to her, Francine smiled and said "Hi!" Dr. Gray nearly fell over backwards. When she regained her composure she said "No! This is not the mattress girl (mattress girl was the name they had given Francine in Chicago)! You're trying to trick me. This is someone else." We assured the doctor that this was the mattress girl. Dr. Gray then shared with us that she was also amazed recently when a little coldwater drowning boy was brought to her clinically dead and he fully recovered. She said that she had to do some rethinking since these two experiences.

On one of our monthly visits to see Dr. Brown for Francine's check up, we were told that her Phenobarbital level was below the therapeutic level and would need to be increased. Jane and I didn't want to do this, thinking we could make a "junky" out of her for the remainder of her life. We decided to take her to the neurologist for another opinion.

Prior to talking to the neurologist, we prayed for a good outcome, as we did on many occasions. I made a mental list of the reasons why we didn't want to increase her medication, the greatest of which was she never had any seizures. I told the neurologist that we were against Dr. Brown's advice to increase Francine's Phenobarbital dosage. Before I could give any reasons, the doctor said "I agree with you. In fact, we'll put together a plan to take her off it completely." And so we did! What a relief! Another step forward!

On the next visit to Dr. Brown, I told him that we took Francine off the Phenobarbital under the Neurologist's plan. I then asked him why we should continue to bring Francine to visit him as he was not doing anything for her. He gave an honest answer, "we're learning from her." I said "in that case, you can pay her for seeing her in the future." That was the last visit to Dr. Brown. We didn't need a monthly reminder of his incompetence.

While we still lived in Michigan, a young lad who lived up the street from us had a dirt bike accident which left him brain injured. Jane went to visit his parents to give them encouragement and offer help in any way. In their discussion they mentioned that the doctor wanted to cut the muscles in their son's arms and legs. Jane tried to talk them out of it, but they went with the doctor's advice. It was unfortunate in that we would later see this boy walking down the street dragging one leg and having one arm flailing out of control. We don't know if he ever improved as we moved out of the State. It did help to reinforce our belief that we did the best for Francine by refusing to let them cut her muscles.

The company and the people that I worked for were very good to me. The division Vice-President wrote a memo stating I was to have all the time off I needed with pay to take care of Francine's problems. I had always received excellent performance reviews and salary increases with several promotions through the years. Shortly after Francine was out of the hospital, my boss received a promotion and a transfer. I was promoted to what would be considered the number two position at the plant.

I began to have some disagreements with my new boss and they came to a head one day over an issue of employee treatment. It all happened as if I was not in control. As I later came to believe, God had a better plan for us and wanted us to move.

Francine shortly after coming home, with one of her prayer warriors and brother Craig in the background

Francine two summers after coming home

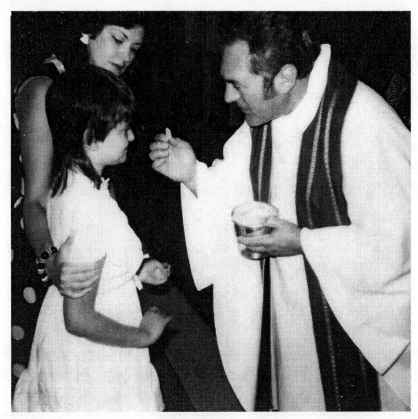

Francine receiving her first communion in Michigan with her mother

Chapter 11

In the Granite State

I ended up taking a job in New Hampshire's Monadnock region. The move was good for me in that I had a less stressful job working with a good group of people. Jane liked it because of better shopping and less severe winters. It was not a big issue for Steve, our oldest son, as he was attending college away from home. It was a little difficult for our youngest son, Craig, as he was in high school. But he soon adjusted, met a nice girl in school and eventually married her.

It was a great move for Francine. We were just a few miles from the highly reputable Crotched Mountain Rehabilitation Center where they specialized in educating and rehabilitating children with disabilities. The school system was also much more progressive. Francine's daily bus ride time was cut from three hours to twenty minutes.

Francine commuted to Crotched Mountain for three years. She was the only commuter that they had as all the others stayed on campus. Crotched Mountain had a full staff of trained teachers, therapists and health care personal to attend to the needs of kids and young adults with disabilities. The pediatrician that cared for the students at Crotched Mountain told us that he wished all his patients were as healthy as Francine. She wasn't on any medications other than for common short term illnesses. Both the Crotched Mountain Rehabilitation Center and the Rehabilitation Institute of Chicago cared for patients that were much more handicapped than Francine. Visits to these places taught us to count our blessings. No matter how distressful your situation seems, there is always someone in a worse situation.

Francine grew into a young lady during those years and continued to slowly improve on her long road to recovery.

When Francine turned fifteen, a representative from the school system approached us suggesting that Francine attend the regular high school in an integrated class room setting. We believed the major motive was to save the school district money but that was fine with us as we were eager to have Francine spend more time with "regular" kids. Some of the kids with disabilities had bad behavior problems and we did not want Francine emulating them. The teacher that Francine would have was described to us as a "free-spirited woman". We did not know what was meant by that, but we later found out.

Margaret Sauvain (Maggie as we affectionately called her) was a person who didn't have the words "can't do" in her vocabulary. She did everything in the book (and a few things that were not in the book) to get the most out of Francine. Maggie got Francine into therapeutic horseback riding, Special Olympics, hiking, gardening and all sorts of extra-curricular activities.

In September of 1990, Maggie writes in her Individualized Education Plan (IEP):

"Francine has blossomed, socially, as a result of being in almost constant contact with her age-appropriate peers. She initiates and responds with "hi" and "bye", both verbally and with gesture, many times using people's names. She responds to yes and no questions more reliably each day and points to pictures to choose activities."

"Computer activities appear to give her the most pleasure and success. She chooses these activities even over lunch! Her independence is increasing on the computer, and she can be left unattended to continue her work for more than 5-10 minutes, now."

"Physically, Frankie has made significant gains. She runs and can hike for at least 3 miles, with assistance, over rough terrain. She is still less free in movements of the right side and nearly always transfers objects to her left hand to do a task. She exhibits some spatial and perceptual confusion and often takes seconds or minutes to begin a motor task."

"Francine seems to learn new things more slowly and by frequent and consistent repetition. She is sometimes successful at modeling motor tasks but usually needs HOH (hand over hand) assistance for initial tries. She initiates quite a lot of vocalization with rhythm and inflection. However, most of her attempts are not easily understandable. She is saying words and sentences that we can understand more frequently. Francine does not seem able to imitate sounds or words on command, outside of certain social situations ("hi," "bye"). She becomes self-conscious and confused when asked to repeat things most of the time or says one of her frequently used "words-for-any-occasion" (baol, caw). Sometimes, she lowers her head and eyes or laughs to indicate her confusion or frustration at not being able to respond."

"There is much more to this young lady than I have been able to unlock, I am sure! I look forward to your assistance in facilitating Francine's growth as a total human being into her approaching adulthood."

Three years later Maggie writes in her IEP:
"Francine is currently attending Horticulture 1 and receiving a grade of C. She is in Oceanography with P/F and is receiving P. She is working at two community job placements quite successfully 5 hours per week. Francine has been using more verbal communication lately and is more able to be understood. She is reluctant to use facilitated communication as much but does on tests and quizzes to verify verbal responses. Francine continues to be cheerful and generally out-going in social situations. She has made some progress with self-care and independent skills."

"Francine is an enthusiastic learner! Sometimes she needs reminding to listen and focus on teacher or task at hand. Having advance notice for quizzes and exams, or even having an extra day to complete them is helpful, as she is distracted in classroom by others talking or moving about. As much as possible, Francine should be treated and interacted with like any other student. Physical tasks take her longer and may have a delayed response. Allowing her to feel unhurried gets the best results. Keeping a smile on your face usually is a good accompaniment to patience. Once her trust is gained a firm, but gentle insistence may be used to gain compliance."

Maggie brought Francine to Special Olympics several times. Twice she was entered into the snowshoe races. Francine's gait was perfect for walking or running on snowshoes and she had been on snowshoes when she was a little girl as I had snowshoes for the entire family in Michigan. She could easily have taken first place in the contests. However, when she got way out ahead of the other participants, she would stop and let them catch up. She wanted to be with the group in spite of the cheering and encouragement from the sidelines. She did not take first place but, like all the other participants, she was a winner. Francine participated enthusiastically and was pleased to be with the other kids and her special friend and teacher, Maggie.

Therapeutic horseback riding was another activity that Maggie got Francine into. She loved it! It helped her posture and self-confidence. She had always loved horses like many young girls. She still does horseback riding once a week as weather permits. The place that she now rides is building an indoor arena and she will soon be able to ride all year around.

Of all the people that have worked with Francine, Maggie stands at the top. Francine loved her in a special way (although Francine loves nearly everybody). To this day she connects women that she especially likes to Maggie, calling them Maggie until she can pronounce their name. We still keep in touch with Maggie.

After nine years in New Hampshire I left for a job in Louisiana. Again, I believe God was behind this move. So in 1995 we left New Hampshire. Francine was graduating from high school so her life would be changing anyway and she would no longer have Maggie to help her. Our sons were both married and were on their own so we felt they did not have a need for us to live nearby.

Francine with her Uncle Earl at the family camp in Michigan

Francine on our 4-wheeled ATV in New Hampshire

Francine swimming at Crotched Mountain

Francine being confirmed in her faith at Crotched Mountain

Francine with her friend Cheryl at Graduation
from Central High School in New Hampshire

Francine with teacher Maggie at the Special Olympics

Francine snowshoe racing and receiving her medal

Francine therapeutic horseback riding

Chapter   12

Time with the Cajuns

We had heard of all the negative things about Louisiana: the high crime rate, the corruption, the filth, lack of zoning, poorly educated people, the heat, the high humidity, etc. So we were somewhat apprehensive about moving there. Some of our apprehension was lifted however when we made a week's visit for an interview. We really came to like the people with their friendliness and hospitality. We would be living about an hour's drive southwest from downtown New Orleans near Bayou Lafourche in Cajun country. I would have a ten minute drive to work.

I lived in Louisiana for a few months before I could find a place to rent that was big enough to hold our furniture as we did not like the idea of putting the furniture in storage. We had looked at the few houses that were for sale but were not satisfied with any of them and therefore we would rent a home that we figured would be temporary. One of the customer services representatives at the mill found a rental house in her neighborhood that was unique and very suitable. It was a Sears & Roebucks house, built when a house could be ordered through the catalog.

There was an advantage for Francine living here in that she was allowed to attend school for another year because the State laws were different. At school she bonded with one of the aids similar to how she bonded with Maggie. Miss Pauline was not only Francine's friend at school, but Francine became a part of her family and we had Miss Pauline as one of Francine's care-givers. Over the eight years we spent with the Cajuns, numerous families "adopted" Francine. The warmth and friendliness of the people in this area of the country helped an already sociable young woman to become even more out-going.

We built a new home in the small community of Gheens (pronounced Gains). I was asked a number of times, "Mr. Dan, why did you choose to live in Greens? Everyone else who comes down from the North decides to live in the city like New Orleans, Houma, or Thibodaux, particularly if they have an important job". I would truthfully tell them "I'm a country boy who likes country people". My attitude helped in quickly becoming part of the community.

The house was built by a family that lived nearby; the senior Mr. Breaux, several of his sons (he had six), some grandsons, and a nephew. The Breauxs quickly adopted us into their family. With such a large family, what's a few more? We were included in all their family functions, which were many, and we often had them at our home for swimming and cookouts.

All the Breaux men were handsome, friendly and caring guys. They all gave Francine special attention sitting and kidding with her and giving her hugs. She loved them all but her favorite was Dean. She would hold her hands out to him and call "Dean, Dean" until she got to him or he came to her. She would recognize his white pickup from miles away picking it out from the hundreds of other white pickups in the area. It was amazing that she could do that. We couldn't tell it was him until he got close. She did the same when she would see my truck off at a distance recognizing it long before anyone else. She would say "Paw Pee" which is the name she uses interchangeably with Daddy.

Along with her exceptionally good sight, was her keen hearing and knowledge of what was happening in her surroundings. When we went shopping, I would often go off to look at items that wouldn't be of interest to Jane. When I came back I would try to sneak up on Jane and Francine to surprise them. I was very seldom successful. Even though I knew where they were or, about where they were, Francine would see me first and alert her mother with laughter.

The family room in our home in Louisiana was to the back side of the house, and when someone came to the front, they could not be seen. When ever someone would drive up to the front of the house, Francine would say something like "oh, oh" and alert us. We would ask if someone was here, if they were, Francine would tell us "yes". It was rare that either Jane or I heard the car drive up unless it had a loud muffler. She was better than a watchdog.

Another amazing incident demonstrating her awareness of her surroundings took place one day when we were returning to our car in the mall's parking lot. We opened the doors (they were unlocked) to get in, but Francine refused to get inside. We didn't know what was wrong. Looking around, we saw some items in the car that did not belong to us and wondered how they got there. After a few moments we realized this was not our car! How did she immediately know that? We had parked several spots further down the lot. The car we were about to enter was the very same model, year and color as ours.
Francine had many fun activities in Louisiana. We purchased a new 4-wheeled ATV and rode all over with it. Besides driving on the

thirty acres that we purchased, we became like everyone else in the community and often times used it instead of the car to visit our friends. Francine would cheer and shout as we rode. She waved to everyone we passed and they returned waves and smiles. Everyone in the community got to know and love Francine.

We had a beautiful pool, and with the long, hot summers Francine had many opportunities to swim. She also was able to do some horseback riding. We took her to a few dances which she thoroughly enjoyed and having some of "her Breaux men" in the band added to her excitement. She clapped for the band, swayed to the music in her chair and got up to dance with us and her friends. We were surprised when she got up for one dance without us noticing and was dancing with a young stranger. She became embarrassed when we began to watch her and she quit for the evening.

Her caregivers often took her to lunch and "bumming around" which was termed "roday" by the Cajuns.

I opted for an early retirement and we purchased a motor home for traveling back to New Hampshire to visit our sons and their wives and our one and only new grandchild at the time. Francine loved traveling in the motor home. The motor home being high off the ground and having large windows presented a great view of all that we would pass. I didn't have to worry about finding a place to stop to go to the bathroom, eat or sleep.

We also took a couple of trips in the motor home to Florida where we attended motor home rallies and visited Disney World. Francine was thrilled with the rides at Disney and, in particular, the shows. Her favorite was the Lion King which put her into tear of enjoyment. We had to see that show at least twice during each visit. We felt that she was just too overwhelmed during the first showing to fully appreciate it.

As our son Craig and his wife Marion provided us with a second beautiful grandchild, we were drawn back to New Hampshire. We now had a grandson and a granddaughter. After living in Louisiana for several years it was our intention of staying there for our retirement years but we felt our family needed us, so we moved back to picturesque New Hampshire. We would have liked to have taken our adopted families with us.

Francine loves to be with her brothers, their wives and her nieces and nephews which total four at this writing. As the grandkids become a little older and have more interaction with Francine, the more they enjoy entertaining her with their antics. Francine also loves babies and whenever she is out and sees them, will stop and say" hi." This usually brings a smile and a "hi" from their parents.

The move again proved to be good for Francine in many respects. We were not aware of it at the time, but New Hampshire had much better programs and services for the disabled than Louisiana. In Louisiana we received a small allowance from the State for respite care and that was all, other than the federally mandated Medicaid which Francine did not use much because she basically had no medical problems. After being on a waiting list for a short period of time, Francine began to receive twenty hours a week of caregiving, a respite allowance and assistance with some development programs including regular therapy and therapeutic horseback riding. She received these benefits and we received guidance from a very helpful and caring Community Services Council.

Francine has since bonded with her most recent caregiver, Billie, who is much like Francine: a loud, out-going, fun-loving woman. Besides taking Francine out to lunch, Billie has taken her on such things as trips to the fair, train rides, a hay ride, to the zoo and swimming. As with other caregivers, Billie has helped Francine to be more independent; making her bed, picking out her clothes, dressing and undressing, etc. Francine gets exited when we tell her Billie is coming or Raven (Billie's daughter) is coming. Raven often polishes Francine's finger nails for her. Francine thinks it's great to have her nails polished and shows them off to everyone.

We continue to see small improvements in Francine. People who have not seen her for several years have particularly noticed a difference. They generally say that she is talking so much more or they can understand more of what she is saying. An example of an improvement that we noticed is that until a year ago, she could not push a shopping cart down the isle of a store without running into things. Now she has no problem keeping it straight and pushing it forward when appropriate.

We don't know what the future holds for Francine – Will she continue to slowly progress? Will she have more miracles? Will there be medical breakthroughs that would enable more healing? Whatever might happen we know that Francine will continue to spread joy to many others by her cheerful greetings and the love of God that radiates through her.

Francine on her own new 4-wheeler in Louisiana

Francine with friend and caregiver, Sarah, in Louisiana

Francine with her friend Ryan in Louisiana

Francine kissing her good friend and caregiver, Holly, in Louisiana

Francine with her love, Dean, his daughter,
Meggie, and you-know-who

Francine with her "good-timing" friend Evelyn during Mardi Gras

Francine with Miss Pauline and husband Murphy

Francine giving Winnie the Pooh a kiss at Disney World

Francine with Billie, her latest caregiver and friend

Francine on a boat ride on Lake Winnipesaukee in New Hampshire

Chapter   13

A Special Gift

Chapter 13   A Special Gift

Over the years, many people have come up to us and told us how much Francine has uplifted them and brightened their day. We notice that when we go places with Francine, her award-winning smile and bubbly personality brings a smile to many faces in return, but her ability to touch others extends further. Francine has the gift of knowing when people are hurting inside particularly those suffering from depression. She reaches out to them and is an instrument in bringing them joy and healing!

The first time we noticed this gift of hers in action, was one day when we were shopping at the mall in New Hampshire. There was a big, tough and mean looking biker standing in front of one of the shops, evidently waiting for a buddy inside the shop. He looked as if he could "chew you up and spit you out in minute" if you crossed him.

Mothers would grab the hand of their children as they passed him by. Everyone gave him a wide berth, being sure not to go too close. But not Francine, she hurriedly walked straight up to this mean guy, hands outstretched with a big smile and an enthusiastic "Hi". She admired the biker's clothing and the metal, chains and earrings that adorned him. She looked into his eyes with her loving smile. He stared back at her with a smile coming to his face. As he continued to smile, tears came down his face. He didn't say a word. Maybe he didn't know what to say or, more likely, he was all choked-up by Francine's love for him. As we walked away we said, "She likes you and all your paraphernalia". The big "tough guy" continued to watch Francine with tears on his face as we went our way.

It is only fitting that most of the time her special gift is used in church. While we lived in Louisiana our home was just diagonally across the street from the church we attended. There was en elderly couple that always sat at the end of one pew which we would pass each week. This couple could take first place in a Mr. & Mrs. Grumpy contest. They appeared to be mad at the world, never smiling. One morning as we passed by them Francine gave them her big smile and wave. They looked astonished as if to say, "Why is she smiling and waving to us?"

The next week Francine did the same thing, only this time Mr. & Mrs. Grumpy cracked a tiny smile. This continued for several weeks. The second week got a larger smile. The third week added a little wave and greater smile. Finally, they were all smiles and waves. They looked for Francine every week and watched her frequently during the services. They smiled through the entire service from then on. Francine most definitely changed their lives! They could now be called Mr. & Mrs. Smiley rather than Mr. & Mrs. Grumpy. Then we no longer saw them! I believe the old gentleman died and his wife moved.

There was a man that attended our church that we knew suffered from depression. One Sunday he was in the front pew kneeling, his head bent down and his eyes staring at the floor. He sure appeared dejected and depressed. As we were returning back to our seats, Francine made a diversion from our normal route. She walked up to him and touched his hand. He was not aware of her approach until she touched him. She was wearing her contagious smile. When he looked up a huge smile came across his face. You could see the depression lifting from him. They held hands for a moment smiling at each other, not saying a word. Then Francine turned and went back to her seat with me.

In the present church that we attend, an elderly lady often sat behind us. Francine would periodically turn and smile at her and reach back and hold her hand. We saw how much this lady enjoyed Francine's attention. When we would come into church she would gesture for us to come and sit by her. One day after the services, Jane talked to the woman. She told Jane that she had terminal cancer and it was depressing her severely. She went on to say that being with Francine had really uplifted her and how much she looked forward to seeing her each week. What a great gift to give to a dying woman!

These are a few of Francine's special touches that I saw personally. How many others were there that I did not witness or pickup on? How did she know these people were depressed and needed some healing?

Many people came to know us through Francine. They know us as Francine's parents. We are well aware that when people see Francine they ask around wanting to know who that handicapped pretty young woman is that is so cheerful and friendly. Often times they don't recognize her as handicapped until they observe her for a while.

Francine can lull a person into thinking that she is not aware of what is going on about her. She understands everything and she comes out with some amazing and often times humorous comments. Most of the time she is uninhibited in speaking out and will say exactly what she feels.

One of those humorous events happened in church one Sunday morning. There was a visiting priest who started his sermon by walking down the isle holding up his hand saying "Look, I'm wearing a wedding band. Does that mean that priests can now get married?" Francine shouts out, "No way!" It was surprising to everyone that someone would respond let alone yell it out in a normally reserved Catholic church. There were giggles and laughter from the congregation. Many of the people knew that it was Francine that shouted. The priest was happy that someone responded to him, and it was the correct answer.

I often think what a tragedy and loss to the world it would have been if we had pulled her feeding tube and "let her go" as we were so strongly urged to do. I also think of people like Terri Schiavo and wonder how many more people they could have touched with their love if they had been allowed to live. And could they have progressed further if they were given the aggressive care like we gave to Francine? My thoughts about Terri were confirmed after listening to her brother Bobby Schindler speak. He said that Terri was progressing until the therapy was stopped. His description of her condition was significantly different than what was reported in the news media. I personally didn't need a report of her condition, I could see it in her eyes and smile.

I recently read the book "A Life That Matters" written by the Schindler family. It particularly angered me as I could relate it to Francine. It is not too far fetched to believe that an activist judge could have put the fate of Francine into the hands of a medical expert like Dr. Gray, taking Francine's care and future out of the hands of the parents that loved her. The world would have been deprived of the love and joy that Francine brings to all. The judge and Terri's husband who controlled her fate cast a dark cloud over the dignity of life and what this Country use to stand for; life, liberty and the pursuit of happiness.

We have talked to Francine a few times about what she remembers from her hospital stay. We needed to be careful in that it upsets her to hear discussion regarding the problems she went through. From answering "yes" or "no" questions, it appears that she remembers nothing about her early days in the hospital but does remember the later part of her hospitalization. Francine also indicated to us that she had died and saw Jesus and His mother, Mary. We believe God sent Francine back to us through Mary. His plan was to use Francine to bring her family and others closer to Him!

There are two young men that also attend our church that are more severely handicapped than Francine. One is wheelchair bound and the other is bed ridden. They certainly have an impact on the community if for no other reason than to remind us of how fragile our health and lives are. We should live our lives loving and caring for others remembering that each one of us has a distinct purpose in life.

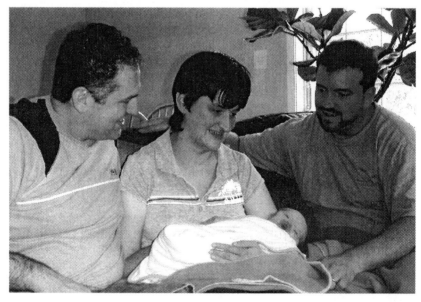

Francine with her brothers Steve and Craig and her new niece

Francine with Mom and Dad

Chapter 14

Conclusions and Advice

My industrial training in report writing compels me to write conclusions and recommendations or advice gained from this experience with Francine. I hope it is helpful not only to those who may have to go through a similar experience as us, but to all who read this story of facing the trials and tribulations in their own lives. May they be strengthened by faith and believe in everyday miracles.

The first conclusion
If you believe in miracles, you will see them. If you don't believe in miracles, you will probably never see one. I use to believe miracles happened to other people in other places such as holy shrines, but now I know they can happen to anyone at any place.

Any one or even a few of Francine's miracles could be explained away as the doctors made mistakes in their prognoses, but time after time they were wrong. I have a hard time believing that these doctors and specialists were so often wrong. These are not ignorant people.

Since Francine's ordeal, we have witnessed other dramatic healings and miracles in other lives and families. If you want to see miracles, your best chance is to associate with other believing people. You won't see too many in the bars.

So my advice is pray, pray and pray some more. Pray with expectation and confidence. Get other people to pray with you or for your intention. Don't just pray for healing. Pray for guidance and confirmation from God. The many decisions and recovery techniques that Jane and I made or used were guided from above. They had to be! We weren't smart enough to challenge the doctors and specialists on our own, nor think-up the various "tricks" to help in Francine's recovery.

Use some caution regarding whom and how prayers are said. We attended a conference on one occasion where some young folks, probably in their late teens, sat behind us and were observing Francine. When the conference ended, they asked if they could pray with Francine. We were happy to let them do so. They began by trying to do an exorcism on her, yelling at Satan to come out and loosen her tongue. I immediately stopped them. There is a Satan and he does horrific damage, but Francine was not demonically possessed. Another example of people being misguided occurred

111

when we had brought Francine to a reputable center for therapy. They laid their hands on her trying to tap into Francine's "inner body energies" to heal her. Jane and I also discontinued this technique as we felt it was anti-Christian.

The second conclusion
Doctors and other health care professionals try doing what is best for their patients. Whether they are inexperienced or just over worked, they sometimes don't make the best decisions. They have a different perspective than you. This is your loved one. To them it may be just another number. They may have some personal problems affecting their work. In some cases, the doctors are learning from you and your loved ones.

The healthcare system has difficulty weeding-out poor doctors. We experienced one doctor covering up for other doctors. It is not my intention to unduly scare people, but simply to prepare you for the unexpected. We dealt with many excellent doctors who did a great job.

You need to watch over your family member or friend when they enter a hospital. Ask questions. Any competent doctor would be willing to answer them. Hopefully, your primary care physician whom you know and trust is involved (This was one thing we were lacking). If possible check on the reputation, particularly of any surgeons that may be operating on them. Do some research. Go for a second or even, a third opinion.

The third conclusion
There was an ample amount of pessimistic attitudes that we encountered. Some of it no doubt comes from the idea that it is not helpful to give too much encouragement for fear of a big let-down when the optimistic prognosis does not materialize. Perhaps a lack of knowledge or faith plays a part. The major problem with not being optimistic is that you may not entertain all your options for the fullest recovery possible.

If we didn't believe Francine would walk again, we would have let her muscles be cut and would not have worked as hard to get her walking and she may have never walked. If we didn't believe Francine would eat again, we wouldn't have worked so hard to get her to eat and she may have been on a feeding tube the remainder of her life. Where there is a will, there is a way.

So, be optimistic yet realistic. It will encourage you to work harder towards the healing of your loved one. It also aids God in doing His will for you. You heard the saying "God helps those who help themselves".

The fourth conclusion

Jane and I supported each other through the entire ordeal with Francine. When one was down, the other was up. When one was up, the other was down. Not only did we support each other emotionally, but we came to an agreement on all the decisions regarding Francine which gave us the confidence that we were doing the right thing regardless of what we were being told. It would have been a disaster for both us and Francine if we did not have each other to lean on or to discuss problems and solutions.

Other support came from family, friends and strangers who called or came to visit Francine while in the hospital or at home during her recovery. They all gave positive, uplifting support. A support system is needed but not a negative one as was put forth by the psychologist at the hospital whose aim was to take away our hope.

Should any difficulty, let alone a tragedy strike your family, hopefully you have a spouse that you can lean on to keep each other sane and proceed with all that is necessary for keeping your health while overseeing the treatment and recovery of your family member. If you're single or don't have a supportive spouse, get another family member or close friend to team up with. Maybe you could use some help from a good psychiatrist or psychologist, although I'm personally skeptical of them. However, the best support system is from God.

The fifth conclusion

We have experienced the happiness and joy on a regular basis that a handicapped daughter has brought us and many others. With Francine's disability we have been brought into closer contact with other mentally handicapped children and adults. In most cases they are loving, happy and humorous people that are fun to be around. They bring something special into this world that others are unable, or refuse to bring.

It is a shame that many people look at the handicapped believing that they don't have a "quality" life when in fact their lives have more quality than many "normal" people. Their love is usually unrequited and unlike many, they give more than they receive. They generally are not burdened down with all the cares and frustrations of the world.

I urge everyone to be involved with the handicapped, particularly those with mental disabilities, to experience the love and joy they radiate. Mercy killing such as pulling feeding tubes and assisted suicide should be stopped. You can never be sure of what the future might bring or what God might do. All life is precious from conception until natural death.

Thank you Lord Jesus for being such a good God!!!

May the hearts and souls of each reader be inspired!

Printed in the United States
73381LV00004BA/259-549

9 781933 899817